Profiles of the Presidents

BENJAMIN HARRISON

★ ★ ★

Profiles of the Presidents

BENJAMIN HARRISON

by Robert Green

Content Adviser: Anne Moore, Librarian, President Benjamin Harrison Home, Indianapolis, Indiana

Reading Adviser: Dr. Linda D. Labbo, Department of Reading Education, College of Education, The University of Georgia

Compass Point Books
3109 West 50th Street, #115
Minneapolis, MN 55410

Visit Compass Point Books on the Internet at *www.compasspointbooks.com*
or e-mail your request to *custserv@compasspointbooks.com*

Editors: E. Russell Primm, Emily J. Dolbear, Melissa McDaniel, and Catherine Neitge
Photo Researcher: Svetlana Zhurkina
Photo Selector: Linda S. Koutris
Designer: The Design Lab
Cartographer: XNR Productions, Inc.

Library of Congress Cataloging-in-Publication Data
Green, Robert, 1969–
  Benjamin Harrison / by Robert Green.
      p. cm. — (Profiles of the presidents)
  Summary: A biography of the twenty-third president of the United States, discussing his personal life, education, and political career.
  Includes bibliographical references and index.
   ISBN 0-7565-0270-5 (hardcover : alk. paper)
   1. Harrison, Benjamin, 1833–1901—Juvenile literature. 2. Presidents—United States—Biography—Juvenile literature. [1. Harrison, Benjamin, 1833–1901. 2. Presidents.] I. Title. II. Series.
   E702 .G74 2003
   973.8'6'092—dc21   2002153300

Table of Contents

★   ★   ★

NOTE: In this book, words that are defined in the glossary are in **bold** *the first time they appear in the text.*

Big Dreams

★　★　★

President Benjamin Harrison looked as dignified and solid as the White House itself. He was only five feet six inches tall, making him shorter than every other president except James Madison. However, he was a confident leader.

Harrison did not try to make people like him. He was not good at chatting with people, and he sometimes made them feel uncomfortable. He often drummed his fingers on the table while others were talking. Some people mistook his lack of patience for arrogance. Harrison was so cold in dealing with members of Congress that some called him the "human iceberg."

Still, people thought highly of President Harrison. He was the grandson of a former president. Everyone who knew him said that he was an honest man. They believed that he was trying hard to make the United States a better nation.

Harrison wanted great things for the United States. When he became president in 1889, the country already

◄ *Benjamin Harrison served as the twenty-third president of the United States.*

stretched across North America, from the Atlantic to the Pacific Oceans. As president, Harrison began to look beyond these shores. He dreamed of the United States becoming a world power. The little president had big ideas.

A Political Family

★ ★ ★

Benjamin Harrison came from a family that had been involved in United States politics since the country's beginnings. Benjamin's great-grandfather, Benjamin Harrison of Virginia, had signed the Declaration of Independence.

Benjamin Harrison's great-grandfather, Benjamin Harrison, was one of the signers of the Declaration of Independence.

Benjamin's grandfather, William Henry Harrison, was a general who led troops against the Shawnee Indians at the Tippecanoe River in Indiana in 1811. "Old Tippecanoe," as he became known, was elected president of the United States in 1840.

Benjamin's father, John Scott Harrison, was a lawyer who had served in the U.S. House of Representatives. However, John didn't have much good to say about politics. He warned Benjamin that politics often attracts men who are not honest or upright. Benjamin's father eventually gave up his law practice to farm the family's land.

Benjamin Harrison, the future twenty-third president of the United States, was born on the family farm in North Bend, Ohio, on August 20, 1833. He was one of nine children. The Harrisons'

◄ William Henry Harrison was the ninth president of the United States.

◄ John Scott Harrison is the only man in U.S. history who was the son of one president and the father of another.

Benjamin was born and raised in North Bend, Ohio. ▲

political connections made them well-known in North Bend. Young Benjamin was aware of the history of his family. From a young age, he developed a rock-steady confidence and the sense that he had an important future.

Benjamin grew up working on the farm and studying at home with tutors. He had a quick mind and did well in his studies. His mother, Elizabeth Irwin Harrison, was a very religious woman. She passed on her strong beliefs to her son. Benjamin was raised a Presbyterian, and he tried to honor the teachings of his religion throughout his entire life.

At age fourteen, Benjamin went away to school at Farmer's College in Cincinnati, Ohio. Two years later, he enrolled at Miami University in Oxford, Ohio. He graduated at the top of his class in 1852.

◀ *Elizabeth Irwin Harrison*

▼ *Harrison attended Miami University in Oxford, Ohio.*

Caroline Lavinia ▲
Scott Harrison
in 1889

While in Oxford, Harrison fell in love with Caroline Lavinia Scott. She was one year older than Harrison and the daughter of the president of the Oxford Female Institute. The two married in 1853, the year after Harrison's graduation. They would eventually have two children.

The young couple lived on the Harrison family farm. Benjamin worked in Cincinnati at the law firm of Storer and Gwynne. He was in training to become a lawyer. In 1854, he passed the exams that allowed him to practice law.

"Little Ben"

★ ★ ★

Harrison opened a law practice in the busy city of Indianapolis, Indiana. He made little money in his early years as a lawyer. However, he earned a reputation for being an honest man with a strong sense of justice.

Despite his father's warnings, Harrison intended to follow in the family footsteps and make a career for himself in politics. He joined the newly formed Republican Party and worked to elect the Republican presidential **candidate**, John C. Fremont, in 1856. Fremont lost the election, but Harrison gained much from the experience. He got a good look at how a

▾ *John C. Fremont lost the presidential election of 1856.*

national **campaign** works, and his own circle of Republican friends grew.

Harrison decided that he should run for public office. He was elected city attorney of Indianapolis in 1857. Then, in 1860, he was elected to be the reporter for the Indiana State Supreme Court. Both jobs allowed Harrison to use his skills as a lawyer. As a court reporter, he was paid well to write explanations of court rulings and to make sure they were published.

Harrison's law office ▾ in Indianapolis

Still, these were minor offices for a politician with big dreams. Harrison needed to meet more people in politics. He next became the secretary of the Indiana Republican Party's central committee. This put Harrison into contact with Republicans throughout the state. It also gave him the chance to gather support for the Republican presidential candidate in 1860.

That candidate was Abraham Lincoln. At that time, the issue of slavery was threatening to tear apart the nation. Slavery was banned in the Northern states but was allowed in the Southern states. Through the years, many political fights had erupted over whether slavery would be allowed in new states in the West. Many Southerners

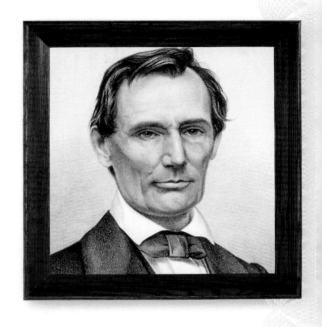

▲ *Abraham Lincoln, the Republican Party's presidential candidate in 1860*

believed that if Lincoln was elected he would end slavery everywhere in the United States. When he won the election, Southern states began seceding, or withdrawing, from the Union. They banded together to form the Confederate States of America.

Lincoln spent his presidency trying to keep the United States from falling to pieces. He did not believe states had the right to leave the Union. Lincoln was willing to use troops to stop them from seceding. This struggle was the Civil War (1861–1865).

To defeat the Confederate troops, Lincoln called on men to join the Union army. Benjamin Harrison was one of those who answered the call. Harrison organized the 70th Indiana **Regiment.** He was made a colonel and was told to get his troops ready for battle.

Harrison was a stern leader, but his men respected his bravery and leadership. They fondly called him "Little Ben" because of his size. A picture of Colonel Harrison from that time shows a long, serious face topped with hair swept back and tucked behind large

Harrison (left) became a brigadier general in the Civil War. He is pictured here with (from left) Union generals Ward, Dustin, and Cogswell.

ears. He had small, flinty
eyes, and a chin that
ended in a bushy beard
that he would wear for
the rest of his life.

Harrison and the
70th Regiment marched
until they met up with
Union General William
T. Sherman, who was
preparing to attack the
Confederate stronghold
of Atlanta, Georgia.
Harrison had studied
hard to learn the art of
war. In battle, both he
and the 70th performed
well. For his leadership
in battle, he was promot-
ed to the rank of briga-
dier general.

Harrison never glo-
ried in his victories on

◄ Harrison was
a stern
military
leader, but
the 70th
Regiment
respected
his courage
in battle.

◄ General
William T.
Sherman led
the Union
army in an
attack on
Atlanta,
Georgia.

the battlefield. He was not a man to celebrate war. For the rest of his political career, however, he would try to make sure the government rewarded **veterans.**

Harrison leading ▶
his troops into the
Battle of Resaca
in May 1864

"Kid Gloves" Strikes Back

★ ★ ★

The Civil War ended in April 1865. Brigadier General Benjamin Harrison returned home to Indianapolis a local hero and a widely respected man. He next turned his attention to his political career. His status as a war hero, devout churchman, and an honest man made him popular with Republican Party leaders. While political scandals were erupting across the United States, Harrison was seen as trustworthy.

Local Republican leaders urged Harrison to run for governor, for Congress, and for just about every other office.

▾ Harrison focused on his political career after the war.

When the Republican candidate for governor of Indiana was accused of corruption, or doing illegal acts for money, he dropped out of the race in 1876. The squeaky-clean Harrison seemed like a good replacement.

Harrison was not much of a campaigner. This was partly because of his modesty. He didn't like to brag about his own accomplishments. This put the Republicans in a tough spot. They had to do all they could to drum up support for him. This left Harrison open to the charge that he was a puppet of the party. The Democratic candidate attacked what he described as Harrison's lack of leadership. He called him "Kid Gloves" Harrison. The attack worked, and the Democrat was elected governor.

Though Harrison had lost the election, many Republicans still had great faith in him. They considered him a sure winner in future campaigns. Harrison became the leader of the Indiana Republican Party and worked to elect other Republican candidates.

In the presidential election of 1880, Harrison threw his support behind Senator James Garfield of Ohio. Harrison was now an important figure in national politics. After winning the election, Garfield offered Harrison a position in his **cabinet.**

Harrison turned him down. He chose instead to run for a seat in the U.S. Senate. At that time, U.S. senators were elected by members of their state **legislature,** not by the people. The Indiana politicians elected Harrison.

Harrison proved to be a much more active senator than people expected after his sluggish campaign in 1876. He believed there was a right and a wrong on most issues. In his six years as a senator, he fought hard for his beliefs and political ideals.

Harrison was a political **reformer.** Reformers wanted to sweep away the corruption that tainted

◄ *James Garfield was elected president in 1880.*

◄ *Harrison during his years as a U.S. senator*

African-Americans like this 1880s cotton worker still did not enjoy the same rights as white Americans, even after the Civil War.

politics, including politicians giving relatives and friends government jobs. They thought people should be hired and promoted based on how well they could perform their jobs and not because of who they knew.

His own sense of fairness made Harrison a natural reformer and also led him to support the rights of African-Americans. The Civil War had freed black Americans from slavery, but they were still a long way from enjoying the rights of white Americans.

While in the Senate, Harrison tried to help veterans, too. Congress passed several **bills** that would have increased payments to Civil War veterans. President Grover Cleveland vetoed these bills. Harrison criticized Cleveland for these vetoes. This helped him win the support of many veterans and their families.

Senator Harrison came up for reelection in 1887. By that time, there were more Democrats in the Indiana legislature than Republicans. Harrison was not reelected. His career as a senator was over. However, Harrison was not ready to give up politics. He announced that he would run for president in 1888 against Grover Cleveland.

▲ *President Grover Cleveland*

United States, 1885
  States
  Territories

Everybody's Second Choice

★   ★   ★

James G. Blaine's political reputation was affected by accusations of corruption. ▾

To have a chance of defeating President Grover Cleveland, Harrison would first have to become the Republican candidate. The favorite in the Republican race was James G. Blaine, who had run for president three times before. Blaine was a reformer who had served in Congress for many years. He was famous for being a powerful speaker. However, Blaine had one big weakness—he had been accused of corruption. The scandal cast a shadow over his presidential bid. Harrison's reputation for honesty made him an appealing choice for many Republicans.

When Republicans held their meeting to choose a presidential candidate, six men wanted the job. Harrison was not the first choice of many of the people attending the meeting. However, he was the second choice for nearly all of them.

▼ *Republicans met in Chicago in 1888 to choose their presidential candidate.*

When Blaine realized that he did not have enough backers to become the candidate, he threw his support behind Harrison. As a result, Harrison—everybody's second choice—became the Republican candidate for president. Levi P. Morton, a New York banker, was chosen as the candidate for vice president.

Harrison faced a difficult job in trying to keep President Cleveland from winning reelection. As was the custom at the time, neither candidate campaigned much. Harrison became known as a front-porch campaigner. Standing at his front door, he spoke to people who gathered around his home. Over the course of the campaign, he gave nearly 90 speeches to 300,000 people from his front porch. He also talked to newspaper reporters who could get his message to a wider audience.

Levi P. Morton became Harrison's running mate in 1888.

For the most part, it was a very gentlemanly campaign. There was one bitter note, however. Democrats
tried to gain support in the South by using Harrison's
wartime leadership against him. They claimed Harrison
was no friend of Southerners.

However, the most important issue in the campaign
was the question of **tariffs.** Harrison wanted to increase
tariffs on foreign products, which would make the products more expensive. He believed that this would help
American companies because people would be more likely

▲ *Crowds gathered at
Harrison's home on
Delaware Street in
Indianapolis during the
presidential campaign.*

to buy the less-expensive American-made goods. Cleveland was against the tariffs. He argued that not having tariffs would give people more choice in what to buy. Cleveland thought tariffs would hurt the economy in the long run.

The election of 1888 proved to be one of the closest in American history. The final tally showed that Grover Cleveland had won more votes than Harrison. He had won the popular vote, but a president is not elected by the direct vote of the people.

Instead, votes in the electoral college decide who becomes president. Each state is awarded electoral votes based on its population. Harrison narrowly won some states with large populations, such as New York and Illinois. This gave him all the electoral votes from these states. Thus, even though he lost the popular vote, he had a clear victory in the electoral college. Benjamin Harrison became the twenty-third president of the United States.

◀ Harrison learned about the 1888 election results while seated in the library in his home in Indianapolis.

An Efficient President

★ ★ ★

The new president was sworn in on March 4, 1889, in the pouring rain. The outgoing president, Grover Cleveland, held an umbrella over the new president's head as he took the oath of office. In his speech that day, Harrison promised Americans a "legal deal," which was his term for a fairer, cleaner government.

Benjamin Harrison taking the oath of office ▾

In the White House, Harrison cut a stately figure. He usually dressed in black and wore a bowler, or a top hat. Late in the afternoon, he often took a buggy ride with another government official. The two would have a serious political discussion while enjoying some fresh air. In the evenings, Harrison usually prepared his work for the next day. Harrison knew in detail the duties of each of his cabinet members. When they were away, he could carry on their work himself.

Though Harrison was a serious man, the White House was jumping with life. Three of his grandchildren lived there. The White House overflowed with their dogs and cats and even a goat named Old Whiskers. One time,

▾ Harrison (center) and his cabinet at the White House

Harrison's son
Russell with his
children, one of
the family dogs,
and Old Whiskers
on the lawn of the
White House

President Harrison, top hat and cane in hand, led his grandchildren on a chase down Pennsylvania Avenue after Old Whiskers.

Harrison's first task as president was to appoint new government officials. The Republicans were eager to replace Democrats in the government. They asked the new president to approve one candidate after another. Harrison appointed hundreds of people to government jobs, but he

quickly grew impatient
with the process.

Those who worked
closely with Harrison
knew well how impatient
the president could be.
He often drummed his
fingers on his desk when
talking to visitors. He
made decisions quickly
in an effort to keep
things moving. Even his
closest aides found his
silent stare bone-chilling.
The White House staff
was overheard whispering a new nickname for President
Harrison. They called him "The Iceberg."

▲ *Theodore Roosevelt was an active government reformer during Harrison's presidency.*

Harrison expected government workers to do their jobs
efficiently and without question. Many people he appointed to government posts became enthusiastic reformers. Two
of his appointees, future president Theodore Roosevelt and
Postmaster General John Wanamaker, helped reform the
way government workers were hired and promoted.

In his campaign for reform, Harrison was lucky that sometimes both Democrats and Republicans were calling for changes that would make the United States a fairer place. Members of both parties were criticizing big business. Some American companies had been increasing in size rapidly. They grew and grew until they controlled an entire industry. These companies became known as trusts.

To limit the power of the trusts, Harrison gained support in Congress for the Sherman Anti-Trust Act. This was the first law in American history that limited

A political cartoon ▸ from Harrison's presidency showing the power of big businesses (right) and the need for politicians (left) to pass the Sherman Anti-Trust Act

the power of large compa-
nies. Every president since
Harrison has tried to
balance the interests of
big business with those
of small companies and
individuals.

Harrison had prom-
ised before the election to
raise tariffs in the United
States. To fulfill this
pledge, Harrison worked
to pass the McKinley
Tariff Act of 1890. The
result was that tariffs rose
by nearly 50 percent.
However, this helped the
business leaders whom
the Sherman Anti-Trust
Act took aim at. The tar-

iffs made it easier for large American companies to control their industries. The McKinley Tariff Act resulted in
making the trusts even stronger.

▲ Wall Street, the
nation's financial
center, in the 1890s

During Reconstruction, court cases were heard by mixed juries like the one shown here. Both whites and blacks were allowed to serve as jurors.

Despite this, Harrison was guided by the desire to create a more just society. He wanted everyone to have a chance to succeed. This can be seen in Harrison's support for laws to protect the rights of black Americans.

The period after the Civil War is called Reconstruction. During that period, government officials had to make sure that the old Confederate leaders did not have too much power and that African-Americans were given their rights.

Many Southerners resented the newly freed slaves. They tried to stop black Americans from voting. To

▾ *Freed blacks in the South shortly after the Civil War*

counter this, Harrison proposed putting Southern elections under federal control. The bill failed, but it showed that Harrison was concerned about the fate of African-Americans.

Harrison also appointed black Americans to positions in government. His most famous black appointee was Frederick Douglass. Before the Civil War, Douglass had worked tirelessly to end slavery. After the war, he turned his attention to making sure that African-Americans were given their rights. Douglass was famous for being a moving and powerful speaker—the black community's leading spokesman. Harrison appointed Douglass the American **minister** to Haiti, an island nation in the Caribbean.

Harrison appointed Frederick Douglass minister to Haiti.

Onto the World Stage

★ ★ ★

In the years following the Civil War, Americans were focused on problems at home. By the time Harrison became president, however, they had begun to look outward. The country's growing wealth led many Americans to believe that the United States should play a greater role on the world stage.

Harrison appointed his former rival James G. Blaine to the post of **secretary of state.** Blaine had a lot of experience in this job. He had already served

▼ James G. Blaine served as secretary of state under Harrison.

as secretary of state for Presidents James Garfield and Chester Arthur.

Under Harrison, the secretary of state became a more important job. Harrison and Blaine dealt more often with the governments of other nations. One reason for this was the McKinley Tariff Act. The act made it too expensive for foreign companies to trade with the United States. Harrison worked out trade agreements with other countries that lowered the tariffs.

Harrison wanted to expand America's role around the world. In 1889, he had Blaine organize a Pan-American Conference to meet with other leaders in the **Americas.** Harrison wanted to improve relations with countries in Latin America. A result of this conference was the future establishment of the Pan-American Games. This athletic competition, which is like the Olympics, still exists today.

Harrison also wanted the United States to expand its influence in the Pacific Ocean. This led to conflicts with other nations that were not eager to have new competition in that part of the world. For example, President Harrison stood firm in protecting American fishing rights in the Bering Sea, which is part of the Pacific

◄ Three-time Olympic gold medalist Wilma Rudolph lit the torch at the opening of the Pan-American games in 1987. The games, which still exist today, grew out of a conference started by Benjamin Harrison.

Ocean between Alaska and Russia. The United States clashed with Great Britain and Canada over this issue.

An even more heated exchange erupted among the United States, Germany, and Great Britain over the Samoan Islands in the South Pacific. The three countries argued over control of the islands. The issue was resolved peacefully, but it showed that Harrison was

America supported Meleatoa Tanu (seated) in becoming king of Samoa.

willing to exert American power in
the Pacific.

Harrison also took an
interest in the Hawaiian
Islands in the Pacific. At
that time, Hawaii was
not yet part of the
United States. It was
rich in resources and
its location in the
middle of the Pacific
made it a useful stop-
ping-off point for ships.

When white settlers
overthrew the Hawaiian leader,
Queen Liliuokalani, Harrison sent
150 American marines to protect the settlers. He wanted
the United States to take over the islands. The U.S. Senate
refused to go along with his plan. American control over
Hawaii would have to wait until a later date.

Harrison knew that to become a world power, the United States needed a strong navy. Before the invention of air-
planes, nations used their navies to show off their strength

▲ *Queen Liliuokalani
of Hawaii*

The USS Indiana *was one of the new battleships built during the 1890s.*

around the globe. Harrison convinced Congress to approve the construction of new battleships. He was committed to turning the U.S. Navy into a world-class fighting force.

One problem that the U.S. Navy faced was how long it took to sail from the East Coast of the United States to the West Coast. To sail from one side of the country to the other, ships had to go all the way around South America. To solve this problem, Harrison tried to convince Congress to pay for building a **canal** through the narrow Central American country of Nicaragua. The canal would make the voyage from the Pacific to the Atlantic Oceans weeks shorter. However, Congress refused to approve Harrison's canal plan.

▼ *This photograph from 1910 shows workers digging the Panama Canal, which made travel easier between the Atlantic and Pacific Oceans. Even though Congress did not approve Harrison's plan, a canal was eventually built in Central America between 1904 and 1914.*

As Harrison's term wore on, Congress became more and more hostile to his plans. In the 1890 election, Democrats had won more seats in Congress than Republicans. Even Republican leaders, however, sometimes gave Harrison the cold shoulder.

As Harrison neared the end of his term, he prepared to run for reelection. It would not be an easy race. Congress was controlled by Democrats, and Republicans were not united behind Harrison. Moreover, high prices resulting from the McKinley Tariff Act had turned many voters against Harrison.

Harrison ran against former president Grover Cleveland. It was the first time two presidents had run against each other. This time, Cleveland easily beat Harrison to become the first and only defeated president to win another term.

When Harrison learned that he had lost the election, he told his family that he felt like he was being freed from prison. It was time to go home.

This was also a difficult time for Harrison personally. His wife had died two weeks before the election. Harrison had to adjust not only to a life away from politics, but also to a life without Caroline. In time, he found comfort in

DAILY TERRITORIAL ENTERPRISE

VOL. LXVI

VIRGINIA, NEVADA TUESDAY, NOVEMBER 8, 1892

NO. 265

POLITICAL ANNOUNCEMENTS.

SAMPLE BALLOT.

To vote for a candidate make a cross thus **X** in the square at the right of his name.

FOR PRESIDENT - BENJAMIN HARRISON
FOR VICE PRESIDENT - WHITELAW REID

For Presidential Electors. Vote for three.

BLISS, D. L.	Republican	X
CLEVELAND, A. C.	Republican	X
FARRELL, J. R.	Republican	

FOR PRESIDENT - GROVER CLEVELAND
FOR VICE PRESIDENT - A. E. STEVENSON

For Presidential Electors. Vote for three.

RILEY, B. F.	Democrat	
RYAN, JOS. R.	Democrat	
WINTERS, THEO.	Democrat	

FOR PRESIDENT - JAMES B. WEAVER
FOR VICE PRESIDENT - JAMES G. FIELD.

For Presidential Electors. Vote for three.

BONNIFIELD, M. S.	Silver Party	
POWNING, C. C.	Silver Party	
WREN, THOMAS	Silver Party	

FOR PRESIDENT - JOHN BIDWELL
FOR VICE PRESIDENT JAMES G. CRANFILL

For Presidential Electors. Vote for three.

BANTA, ABRAM	Prohibition	
MOORE, CHAS. F.	Prohibition	
WILSON, WM.	Prohibition	

Representative in Congress. Vote for one.

GARDNER, CHAS. H.	Prohibition	
HAGERMAN, JAS. C.	Democrat	
NEWLANDS, FRANCIS G.	Silver Party	X
WOODBURN, WILLIAM	Republican	

State Board of Regents. Vote for one long one short.

KINKEAD, JOHN H. (short term)	Republican	X
RULE, HENRY R. (long term)	Republican	X
DOUGLAS, Sr. J. F. (short term)	Democrat	
LEMMON, FIELDING (long term)	Democrat	
FISH, HENRY I. (long term)	Silver Party	
MACK, CHAS. E. (short term)	Silver Party	

Justice of Supreme Court. Vote for one.

BELKNAP, C. H.	Silver Party and Democrat	

State Senators. Vote for one.

BOYLE, E. D.	Silver Party	
CANDLER, W. M.	Republican	X

Members of the Assembly. Vote for six.

CRANDALL, C. H.	Republican	X
DOWLING, S.	Republican	X
FOLSOM, F. W.	Republican	X
NEWCOMB, E. A.	Republican	X
PRINGLE, C. H.	Republican	X
WILLIAMS, T. P.	Republican	X
CARAH, H. T.	Silver Party	
LOCHLIN, W.	Silver Party	
LANGAN, J.	Silver Party	
LERNHART, A.	Silver Party	
MONAHAN, F.	Silver Party	
SMITH, G. R.	Silver Party	

For Sheriff. Vote for one.

HUBBS, J. H.	Republican	X
QUIRK, J.	Silver Party	

County Clerk and ex-officio Treasurer. Vote for one.

HATCH, G. W.	Silver Party	
TULLY, W. H.	Republican	X

Recorder and Auditor. Vote for one.

KELLY, J. M.	Silver Party	
NYE, H. A.	Republican	X

District Attorney and Supt of Schools Vote for one.

HUFFAKER, F. M.	Independent	
KNIGHT, E. D.	Republican	X
STEFFAN, A.	Silver Party	

Public Administrator. Vote for one.

BECK, H. S.	Silver Party	
FAY, H. R.	Republican	X

County Commissioners. Vote for one long and one short.

CHATELAIN, E. (short term)	Silver Party	
HEFFRON, T. (short term)	Independent	
KEMP, W. (long term)	Silver Party	
McMILLAN, M. C. (short term)	Republican	X
PRATT, W. H. (long term)	Republican	X
TREWELLA, H. (long term)	Independent	

County Surveyor. Vote for one.

BALL, ROBERT	Republican	X

Justice of the Peace Vote for one.

BARTLETT, B. F.	Independent	
COREY, J. C.	Republican	X
LOBENSTEIN, L.	Silver Party	
PEMBERTHY, J.	Independent	

Constable Township No 1 Virginia. Vote for one.

BRAVIN, R. D.	Silver Party	
HILL, W. J.	Republican	X
WELSH, J. T.	Independent	

School Trustee Vote for two long, two short.

GRACEY, R. (long term)	Republican	X
LIDDLE, W. (short term)	Republican	X
MORGAN, G. H. (long term)	Republican	X
WILBER, H. (short term)	Republican	X
CRANE, T. H. (long term)	Silver Party	
HULLY, T. (short term)	Silver Party	
HUFF, F. (long term)	Silver Party	
MOORE, C. (short term)	Silver Party	

Justice of the Peace Township No 2 Gold Hill Vote for one.

COOK, E. C.	Silver Party	
LOWRY, J.	Republican	X

Constable, Township No. 2, Gold Hill. Vote for one.

CROWLEY, J.	Silver Party	
MARES, T.	Independent	
WADGE, J.	Republican	X

School Trustee Gold Hill Vote one long one short

BOOTH, S. (long term)	Independent	
VASS, J. (short term)	Independent	

E. D. Knight,
District Attorney and ex-officio Sup't of Schools.

W. H. Tully,
County Clerk and ex-officio County Treasurer.

Louis Lobenstein,
Justice of the Peace.
Township No. 1, Virginia City.

Benj. F. Bartlett,
JUSTICE OF THE PEACE.

Wilson Locklin,
Assemblyman.

Thomas Heffron
County Commissioner. (Short Term.)

J. C. Corey,
Justice of the Peace, Township No. 1—Virginia City.

A. Lernhart,
Assemblyman.

J. H. Hubbs,
Sheriff and Assessor.

William Kemp,
Long Term County Commissioner.

Capt. Harry Trewella,
County Commissioner (LONG TERM.)

Albert Steffan,
District Attorney and Ex-Officio Sup't of Schools.

F. M. Huffaker,
District Attorney and Ex-Officio Sup't of Schools.

Thomas Marks,
Constable
Township No. 2—Gold Hill.

E. D. Boyle,
State Senator.

E. A. Newcomb,
Assemblyman.

Samuel Dowling,
Assemblyman.

F. W. Folsom,
Assemblyman.

Chas. Crandall.
Assemblyman.

John M. Kelly,
RECORDER AND AUDITOR.

◄ The front page of a newspaper from November 1892 that shows a sample ballot for the presidential election that year

the company of Mary Scott Dimmick, who was his wife's niece and had served as her secretary. The two married in 1896 and had a daughter the following year.

After moving out of the White House, Harrison continued to work. He gave a series of lectures about

Mary Scott Dimmick became Harrison's second wife in 1896. She was a widow, thirty years his junior.

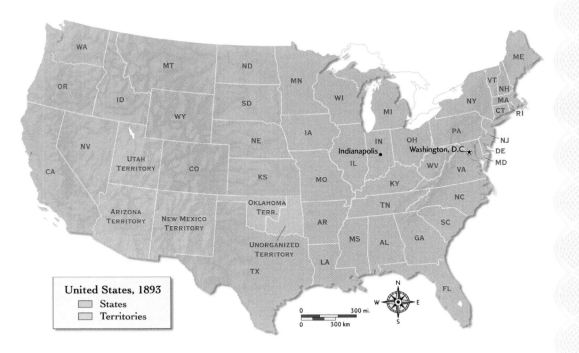

United States, 1893
- States
- Territories

the law. He also helped resolve disputes between countries.

Benjamin Harrison always had a big vision for the United States. Many of his dreams for the nation would later come true. Hawaii became a U.S. territory in 1900. Later, at the urging of President Theodore Roosevelt, a canal was built across Central America. The Panama Canal was completed in 1914.

Benjamin Harrison would not live to see this triumph, however. Little Ben, the last Civil War general to serve as president of the United States, died on March 13, 1901.

Many of Harrison's ideas for America were carried out after his presidency came to an end.

GLOSSARY

★ ★ ★

Americas—the lands of the western hemisphere including North, Central, and South America and the West Indies

bills—proposed laws

cabinet—a president's group of advisers who are heads of government departments

campaign—an organized effort to win an election

candidate—someone running for office in an election

legislature—the part of government that makes or changes laws

minister—an official who represents one country in another country

reformer—someone who tries to make government more honest and efficient

regiment—a military group made up of several battalions

secretary of state—a president's leading adviser in dealing with other countries

tariffs—taxes placed on certain foreign goods entering a country

veterans—people who served in the military

BENJAMIN HARRISON'S LIFE AT A GLANCE

★ ★ ★

PERSONAL

Nickname: Kid Gloves Harrison, Little Ben

Birth date: August 20, 1833

Birthplace: North Bend, Ohio

Father's name: John Scott Harrison

Mother's name: Elizabeth Irwin Harrison

Education: Graduated from Miami University in Oxford, Ohio, in 1852

Wives' names: Caroline Lavinia Scott Harrison (1832–1892); Mary Scott Lord Dimmick Harrison (1858–1948)

Married: October 20, 1853; April 6, 1896

Children: Russell Benjamin Harrison (1854–1936); Mary Scott Harrison (1858–1930); Elizabeth Harrison (1897–1955)

Died: March 13, 1901, in Indianapolis, Indiana

Buried: Crown Hill Cemetery in Indianapolis

PUBLIC

Occupation before presidency:	Lawyer, soldier, public official
Occupation after presidency:	Lawyer, lecturer, writer
Military service:	Brigadier general during the Civil War
Other government positions:	Indianapolis city attorney; reporter for the Indiana Supreme Court; member of the Mississippi River Commission; U.S. senator from Indiana
Political party:	Republican
Vice president:	Levi P. Morton (1889–1893)
Dates in office:	March 4, 1889–March 4, 1893
Presidential opponents:	Grover Cleveland (Democrat), 1888 and 1892; James B. Weaver (Populist), 1892
Number of votes (Electoral College):	5,447,129 of 10,984,986 (233 of 401), 1888; 5,182,690 of 11,767,962 (145 of 444), 1892
Writings:	*This Country of Ours* (1897), *Views of an Ex-President* (1901)

★

Benjamin Harrison's Cabinet

Secretary of state:
James G. Blaine (1889–1892)
John W. Foster (1892–1893)

Secretary of the treasury:
William Windom (1889–1891)
Charles Foster (1891–1893)

Secretary of war:
Redfield Proctor (1889–1891)
Stephen B. Elkins (1891–1893)

Attorney general:
William H. H. Miller (1889–1893)

Postmaster general:
John Wanamaker (1889–1893)

Secretary of the navy:
Benjamin F. Tracy (1889–1893)

Secretary of the interior:
John W. Noble (1889–1893)

BENJAMIN HARRISON'S LIFE AND TIMES

★ ★ ★

HARRISON'S LIFE		WORLD EVENTS

1830

August 20, Benjamin Harrison is born in North Bend, Ohio (below) — 1833

1833   Great Britain abolishes slavery

1836   Texans defeat Mexican troops at San Jacinto after a deadly battle at the Alamo

1837   American banker J. P. Morgan is born

1840   1840   Auguste Rodin, famous sculptor of *The Thinker* (right), is born

1848   *The Communist Manifesto,* by German writer Karl Marx, is widely distributed

HARRISON'S LIFE

WORLD EVENTS

1850

Graduates from Miami 1852
University (below)

Marries Caroline 1853
Lavinia Scott

Becomes a lawyer 1854

1852 American Harriet
Beecher Stowe
(below) publishes
*Uncle Tom's
Cabin*

1858 English scientist
Charles Darwin
(above) presents
his theory
of evolution

HARRISON'S LIFE

Elected reporter 1860
of the Indiana
Supreme Court

Enters the 1862
Union
army as a
colonel (left)

Promoted to brigadier 1864
general (below left)

Runs unsuccessfully 1876
for governor of
Indiana

1860

1870

WORLD EVENTS

1860 Austrian composer
Gustav Mahler is born
in Kalischt (now in
Austria)

1869 The transcontinental
railroad across the
United States is
completed (above)

The periodic table of
elements is invented

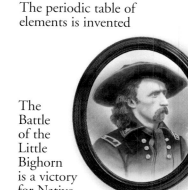

1876 The
Battle
of the
Little
Bighorn
is a victory
for Native
Americans defending
their homes in the
West against General
George Custer (right)

HARRISON'S LIFE

1880

Serves in the 1881–
U.S. Senate 1887

WORLD EVENTS

1882 Thomas Edison builds a power station

1884 Mark Twain (right) publishes *The Adventures of Huckleberry Finn*

1886 Grover Cleveland dedicates the Statue of Liberty in New York

Bombing in Haymarket Square, Chicago (below), due to labor unrest

Presidential Election Results:	Popular Votes	Electoral Votes
1888 Benjamin Harrison	5,447,129	233
Grover Cleveland	5,537,857	168

March 4, is sworn in as 1889
president (below),
becoming the only
grandson of a president
to be president

The Pan-American
Union is created

HARRISON'S LIFE

1890

The Sherman Anti-Trust Act outlaws trusts

The McKinley Tariff Act raises tariffs to record highs

1891

Electric lights are installed in the White House

1892

Caroline Harrison (above) dies

Loses his bid for reelection to former president Grover Cleveland (below)

WORLD EVENTS

1890

1891

The Roman Catholic Church publishes the encyclical *Rerum Novarum,* which supports the rights of labor

1892

American author Walt Whitman dies

Ellis Island in New York Bay becomes a receiving point for U.S. immigrants.

HARRISON'S LIFE

Marries Mary Scott
Dimmick (above) — 1896

Publishes *This Country
of Ours,* which explains
how the federal
government works — 1897

Represents Venezuela
in a border dispute — 1898-
1899

March 13, dies in — 1901
Indianapolis, Indiana

WORLD EVENTS

1893 — Women gain voting
privileges in New
Zealand, the first
country to take such
a step

1896 — The Olympic Games
are held for the first
time in recent history,
in Athens, Greece
(below)

1899 — Isadora Duncan
(below), one of the
founders of modern
dance, makes her
debut in Chicago

1900

UNDERSTANDING BENJAMIN HARRISON AND HIS PRESIDENCY

★ ★ ★

IN THE LIBRARY

Clinton, Susan. *Benjamin Harrison: Twenty-Third President of the United States.* Chicago: Childrens Press, 1989.

Francis, Sandra. *Benjamin Harrison: Our Twenty-Third President.* Chanhassen, Minn.: The Child's World, 2002.

Joseph, Paul. *Benjamin Harrison.* Minneapolis: Abdo Publishing, 2000.

ON THE WEB

Internet Public Library—Benjamin Harrison
http://www.ipl.org/div/potus/bharrison.html
For information about Harrison's presidency
and many links to other resources

The American President—Benjamin Harrison
http://www.americanpresident.org/history/benjaminharrison
To read in-depth information about Harrison

The American Presidency—Benjamin Harrison
http://gi.grolier.com/presidents/ea/bios/23pharr.html
To read a biography of Harrison and his inaugural address

HARRISON HISTORIC SITES
ACROSS THE COUNTRY

The President Benjamin Harrison Home
1230 North Delaware Street
Indianapolis, IN 46202
317/631-1888
To visit the president's former home,
which is now a museum

Crown Hill Cemetery
700 West 38th Street, Lot 13
Indianapolis, IN 46208
317/925-8231
To visit Harrison's grave

THE U.S. PRESIDENTS
(Years in Office)

★ ★ ★

1. **George Washington**
   (March 4, 1789–March 3, 1797)
2. **John Adams**
   (March 4, 1797–March 3, 1801)
3. **Thomas Jefferson**
   (March 4, 1801–March 3, 1809)
4. **James Madison**
   (March 4, 1809–March 3, 1817)
5. **James Monroe**
   (March 4, 1817–March 3, 1825)
6. **John Quincy Adams**
   (March 4, 1825–March 3, 1829)
7. **Andrew Jackson**
   (March 4, 1829–March 3, 1837)
8. **Martin Van Buren**
   (March 4, 1837–March 3, 1841)
9. **William Henry Harrison**
   (March 6, 1841–April 4, 1841)
10. **John Tyler**
    (April 6, 1841–March 3, 1845)
11. **James K. Polk**
    (March 4, 1845–March 3, 1849)
12. **Zachary Taylor**
    (March 5, 1849–July 9, 1850)
13. **Millard Fillmore**
    (July 10, 1850–March 3, 1853)
14. **Franklin Pierce**
    (March 4, 1853–March 3, 1857)
15. **James Buchanan**
    (March 4, 1857–March 3, 1861)
16. **Abraham Lincoln**
    (March 4, 1861–April 15, 1865)
17. **Andrew Johnson**
    (April 15, 1865–March 3, 1869)

18. **Ulysses S. Grant**
    (March 4, 1869–March 3, 1877)
19. **Rutherford B. Hayes**
    (March 4, 1877–March 3, 1881)
20. **James Garfield**
    (March 4, 1881–Sept 19, 1881)
21. **Chester Arthur**
    (Sept 20, 1881–March 3, 1885)
22. **Grover Cleveland**
    (March 4, 1885–March 3, 1889)
23. **Benjamin Harrison**
    (March 4, 1889–March 3, 1893)
24. **Grover Cleveland**
    (March 4, 1893–March 3, 1897)
25. **William McKinley**
    (March 4, 1897–
    September 14, 1901)
26. **Theodore Roosevelt**
    (September 14, 1901–
    March 3, 1909)
27. **William Howard Taft**
    (March 4, 1909–March 3, 1913)
28. **Woodrow Wilson**
    (March 4, 1913–March 3, 1921)
29. **Warren G. Harding**
    (March 4, 1921–August 2, 1923)
30. **Calvin Coolidge**
    (August 3, 1923–March 3, 1929)
31. **Herbert Hoover**
    (March 4, 1929–March 3, 1933)
32. **Franklin D. Roosevelt**
    (March 4, 1933–April 12, 1945)

33. **Harry S. Truman**
    (April 12, 1945–
    January 20, 1953)
34. **Dwight D. Eisenhower**
    (January 20, 1953–
    January 20, 1961)
35. **John F. Kennedy**
    (January 20, 1961–
    November 22, 1963)
36. **Lyndon B. Johnson**
    (November 22, 1963–
    January 20, 1969)
37. **Richard M. Nixon**
    (January 20, 1969–
    August 9, 1974)
38. **Gerald R. Ford**
    (August 9, 1974–
    January 20, 1977)
39. **James Earl Carter**
    (January 20, 1977–
    January 20, 1981)
40. **Ronald Reagan**
    (January 20, 1981–
    January 20, 1989)
41. **George H. W. Bush**
    (January 20, 1989–
    January 20, 1993)
42. **William Jefferson Clinton**
    (January 20, 1993–
    January 20, 2001)
43. **George W. Bush**
    (January 20, 2001–)

INDEX

★ ★ ★

ABOUT THE AUTHOR

Robert Green holds a master's degree in journalism from New York University and a bachelor's degree in English literature from Boston University. He has also studied Chinese in Taiwan.

Green is the author of *Theodore Roosevelt, Woodrow Wilson,* and *Richard Nixon* in this series. He has also written twenty other nonfiction books for young readers, including *Modern Nations of the World: China* and *Modern Nations of the World: Taiwan* and biographies of historical figures including Julius Caesar, Cleopatra, Alexander the Great, Tutankhamun, Herod the Great, and Hannibal.